The beauty of NELSON

Mapua

Photographs by Graeme Matthews

Marahau

The beauty of
NELSON

Published by Photoimage
Blenheim
New Zealand
Phone/Fax: +64 3 570 5655
Email: g.matthews@clear.net.nz
Ptinted in Hong Kong
Photographs copyright © Graeme Matthews
Typeset by Go Ahead Graphics, Christchurch

Hardcover: ISBN 978-0-473-12645-2
Softcover: ISBN 978-0-473-12644-5

Opposite:
Nelson's wild and remote western coastline.

'I was there about September and nothing could be sweeter or more pleasant than the air. The summer heats are not great, and all the English fruits, and grass, and shrubs grow at Nelson with more than English profusion. Every house is neat and pretty. The site is, I think, as lovely as that of any town I ever saw. Merely to breathe there, and to dream, and to look around was a delight.'

Novelist Anthony Trollope wrote those words in 1872, during a visit to New Zealand, and they remain as true today, more than 130 years later. With its mild climate, its stunning sea and landscapes, its fertile soils and its wealth of arts and crafts, Nelson is one of New Zealand's most attractive and popular regions.

Its geographical position gives it a unique mixture of the North and South Islands The warm, sandy beaches are reminiscent of those further north, while the soaring peaks and rivers are distinctively southern. Although a relatively small region, it contains great tracts of astonishing wilderness, much of it lying in three national parks – Abel Tasman, Kahurangi and Nelson Lakes. Then there are the thriving urban centres of Nelson and Richmond; the horticultural and coastal settlements of the three Ms: Mapua, Motueka and Moutere; the justly famous and popular coastline of Golden Bay; and the lakes and rivers of the Murchison/St Arnaud area.

Nelson was fought over by northern and southern Maori as tribe after tribe migrated from the North Island, among them Ngati Mamoe and Ngati Tumatakokiri. It was the latter who, as a result of a misunderstanding, killed four Dutch sailors when explorer Abel Janszoon Tasman sailed into Golden Bay in December 1642. As a result he christened this lovely place Murderers' Bay. Yorkshireman Captain James Cook had a much more peaceful experience when he visited the area on his first New Zealand voyage in 1770.

Northern tribe Ngai Tahu held the Nelson–Golden Bay area for a century before Ngati Toa, under the great chief Te Rauparaha, and other tribes swept down from the north in a series of bruising attacks. By the end of 1830 Ngati Toa and its allies controlled the northern South Island.

The first organised European settlement began when the New Zealand Company, in the person of Colonel William Wakefield, bought more than 80,000 hectares of land in Tasman and Golden Bay from Te Rauparaha. An advance party led by Captain Arthur Wakefield arrived in Nelson Haven in November 1841; the first migrant ship reached the future port early in 1842. The settlement was slow to get under way, owing to economic depression and shortage of usable land, and the clash between Maori and Pakeha at Wairau in 1843 did not help matters, but by the mid-1840s Germans were settling in Upper Moutere and Nelson itself went ahead once the New Zealand Company reduced land prices. In 1857 Golden Bay was the site of New Zealand's first significant gold strike when more than 2000 hopeful miners descended on Collingwood. There were no big finds, however, and the gold was exhausted by 1860.

Now the region earns its living from tourism, fruit of all kinds, timber, award-winning wine and fish. The city of Nelson offers the visitor a rich and appealing blend of cafés, arts and crafts galleries, charming and impressive historical buildings, pleasant parks and walks, a delightful weekend market and, for family fun, magnificent Tahunanui Beach, only minutes from the town centre. Beyond the towns this exciting and lovely region offers an exciting and fascinating variety of landscape, from golden beaches to high mountain lakes, from extraordinary rock formations to lush trees, from wild coasts to tranquil rivers. As Maurice Shadbolt once wrote, 'To know Nelson is to know New Zealand.'

Opposite:
Wharariki Beach just to the west of Cape Farewell is renowned for its extraordinary landscape of islands, rock bridges, caves, arches and headlands, where seals sometimes bask. Wharariki, which is part of Puponga Farm Park, is only a 20-minute walk along a good track from a carpark.

Above:
Famous for its seafood, the Boat Shed Café on Nelson's waterfront is an icon of the town.

Opposite:
Founded in 1842 when 500 settlers arrived on the *Fifeshire*, the *Mary Ann*, the *Lloyds* and the *Lord Auckland*, Nelson (population 43,500), originally called Wakatu, is New Zealand's second oldest city. Queen Victoria bestowed that status in 1858. The compact, easily walked commercial centre is full of art and craft galleries, cafés and restaurants. The busy port, which exports almost three million tonnes of cargo every year from Nelson's forestry sector, fruit growers and seafood processors, is also popular with boaties.

Left:
Surrounded by attractive gardens and trees, Nelson's Christ Church Cathedral overlooks the city from its commanding position on Church Hill at the top of Trafalgar Street. Completed in 1965, and built mainly of Takaka marble, it is the third church building on this site. Church Hill – in Maori Pikimai (climb up here) – played a major role in Nelson's history. Newly arrived settlers were housed here and it was also the site of the post office, the New Zealand Company's storerooms and barracks and the courthouse.

Nelson's name is not the only connection with England's most famous sailor, Admiral Sir Horatio Nelson. The main thoroughfare, lovingly cared for and rich in period detail and bright with flower baskets, is Trafalgar Street, named after the great man's most famous battle. Nile and St Vincent Streets recall other military highpoints. Hardy and Collingwood Streets remember famous admirals, Vanguard and Victory equally famous ships.

Above:
The lovely sweep of Tahunanui (Tahuna) Beach, only minutes from the heart of Nelson city, is always populated by walkers or people simply enjoying the view from a comfortable spot on the sand. With a playground, zoo park, mini-golf, a model railway and a hydroslide, the beach is an ideal family destination. Tahunanui means large sandbank.

Monuments to Nelson's past. The Early Settlers Monuments remembers the European pioneers. A seagull perches on the head of Dutch explorer and navigator Abel Janszoon Tasman (1603–59), who came to New Zealand in 1642. When his two ships, the *Heemskerck* and *Zeehaen*, sailed into Golden Bay, Maori canoes met them and in the ensuing clash, born of cross-cultural misunderstanding, four Dutch sailors were killed. The third monument represents the proud seafaring history of Nelson.

Above:
The Saturday morning market in Nelson's Montgomery Square is a rich hunting ground for those interested in crafts, food, clothing and other delights.

Opposite:
Built in 1855 of cob, handsome Broadgreen House at Stoke, south of Nelson, was home to Nelson department store owner Edmund Buxton, his wife and six daughters. A typical gentleman's residence of its day, it is fully furnished with period furniture – the kitchen is a particular highlight – and set in extensive lawns with notable specimen trees planted by Buxton. At the front of the house is the beautiful Samuels Rose Garden, named after a rose nurseryman who established it for the people of Nelson. Only two families owned the house before it was bought by the city in 1965.

Above:
Nelson is a sailor's paradise. Here a boy launches an Optimist yacht at the Nelson Yacht Club.

Above:
In perfect weather, on sparkling waters, craft of all sizes and shapes sail in the Nelson Yacht Club's 150th anniversary regatta in 2007.

Above:
Isel House, at Stoke, was built about 1850 by Thomas Marsden from Derbyshire, who arrived in the area with his wife Mary in 1842. The original 376-hectare farm, on which Marsden planted a number of trees, has now been reduced to a 6-hectare park that is famous for its spring woodland garden. The eye-catching stone and brick frontage was added by Marsden's son James in the 1880s.

Opposite:
More than 13 kilometres long, Nelson's Boulder Bank looks artificial but is entirely natural, formed of big boulders moved from MacKay Bluff during northerly storms. It is one of the very few examples of this type of breakwater in the world.

Above:
Window on the land of the long white cloud – this arresting *trompe-l'oeil* mural is on Nelson's waterfront.

Above:
The Collingwood Street bridge over the tranquil Matai River in Nelson.

Opposite:
History buffs are drawn to Nelson's South Street, a charming and unspoilt cul-de-sac of workers' cottages that have remained almost unchanged since they were built in the 1860s. Several are available as accommodation.

Above:
This eye-catching monument marks the geographical centre of New Zealand. The wonderful views over the city and beyond make the short but steep walk from the Botanical Reserve well worth the effort. The country's first game of rugby, organised by Charles Monro, was played at the reserve on 14 May 1870. The Nelson Football Club defeated Nelson College two goals to nil.

Above:
A brightly coloured mural promoting peace livens up a wall in Tahunanui.

Above:
Cars and clothes share museum space in Quarantine Road, Annesbrook, on the outskirts of Nelson. The World of WearableArt Awards are now held annually in Wellington but WOW was born in Nelson in 1987 and this museum shows a fabulous range of past winners. The Classic Cars collection contains more than 50 cars and motorbikes.

ANCHOR INN

Opposite:
Immediately identifiable by its landmark windmill, Founders Heritage Park in Atawhai Drive stands on a site that was once a landfill. Opened in 1986, it consists of heritage and replica buildings, some as displays and some as businesses. Handsome Old St Peter's Church was consecrated on 1 October 1874 as St-Peter's-by-the-Strand, because its original site was by Nelson Haven. Interdenominational, it is available for weddings and other Christian services. The Anchor Inn, to the right, was once a favoured and rollicking drinking place for seafarers when it stood on Haven Road in Port Nelson. It was then known as the Clarendon and later became the Glen Rae Guest House. When it was moved to the park and was restored it reverted to the name that appeared on its original plans.

Above:
With a beautifully restored red Hunslet diesel engine in the background, a family group enjoys a jigger ride at Founders Heritage Park. Train rides are also available on occasions.

Above:
Named after Nelson's sister city in Japan, the Miyazu Garden in Atawhai Drive is a traditional Japanese stroll garden, where large boulders, stonework, ponds and stepping stones create a serene and tranquil environment. In spring the cherry blossom is not to be missed.

Opposite:
The unspoilt beauty of Cable Bay estuary, and its walkway, lies only a short distance north of Nelson city. When the Eastern Extension Cable Company opened in February 1876, the eastern terminal of the cable from Australia was located in this bay.

Above:
Nelson is famous for its enticing wineries and vineyards in gorgeous settings and these vines at Appleby near Richmond are no exception. The netting protects ripening grapes from hungry birds. The region is noted for award-winning sauvignon blancs, chardonnays and pinot noirs.

Above:
The decorative wooden Anglican church of St John's, built in 1846 on a hillside in the little settlement of Wakefield, is the oldest church in the South Island and the second oldest in New Zealand after Russell's Christ Church. It is also one of the oldest churches in continuous use. The first service, taken by resident Nelson vicar, the Reverend C.L. Reay, was held on 11 October 1846. The church, which once featured on a Christmas stamp, has been enlarged and renovated over the years. It boasts a particularly fine kauri lining.

Above:
Idiosyncratic scarecrows near Ngatimoti, Lower Moutere, seem to be ready for bed.

Above:
Wine is not the only alcoholic beverage for which the Nelson region is famous. Hops, here being harvested near Ngatimoti at the end of summer, have long been grown in the northern South Island. They are used in the brewing of beer, which is made and sold at a number of popular boutique breweries.

Opposite and above:
The lush green of introduced English trees, especially poplars, and the spiky shapes of indigenous cabbage trees line the highway through the Motueka Valley, which is one of the main entry points to Kahurangi National Park.

Left:
A boy enjoys a river swing at Quinneys Bush Camp on the Motupiko River. The Maori name means a straggling grove or bush area.

Opposite:
The lovely tree-lined Motueka River is famous for its brown trout fishing. The side valleys on its western bank give access to the walks and tramping tracks in the Mount Arthur and Tablelands and to the Wangapeka Track.

Above:
Could this splendid corrugated iron chookhouse, near Tapawera, be the fanciest in New Zealand?

Above:
'La-half-abull' is the title of the unique wood stump carving. There is plenty of outdoor seating on offer at the Kohatu Hotel.

Opposite:
In a perfect mirror image, winter snow on the St Arnaud Range is reflected in the placid waters of Lake Rotoiti in Nelson Lakes National Park. W.T.L. Travers named the mountains after the French commander in the Crimean War, but photographer and mountaineer John Pascoe told of the local name for the peaks, No-Catch-'Em, after the words of a musterer who returned empty-handed when sent to round up sheep on the slopes.

Above:
Traditional wooden dinghies and yachts take part in the annual classic boat regatta held on Lake Rotoiti, which is popular for boating and all water sports. John Sylvanus Cotterell was the first European to see the lake, on 18 January 1843. Its Maori name means small lake. When explorer and geologist Julius von Haast (1822–87) saw the lake in 1860, he praised its 'deep blue waters' which 'reflected the high rocky mountain chains on its eastern and southern shores which, for a considerable height from the water's edge are clad with luxuriant primeval forest'.

Above:
In Nelson Lakes National Park huts at Lake Angelus are dwarfed by the bare rocky slopes of the Angelus Ridge, which soars to over 1850 metres. Established in 1956, the 102,000-hectare park includes beech forest, mountains, streams and lakes. The gateway to the park is the town of St Arnaud, a one- to two-hour drive from Nelson or Blenheim.

Opposite:
Black swans make themselves at home on the edge of Lake Rotoroa (long lake), the largest of the lakes in Nelson Lakes National Park. Less than 500 metres above sea level, Rotoroa is a favourite destination for trout fishers. The first Europeans to see the lake, in 1846, were a group of explorers led by Charles Heaphy.

Opposite:
The tranquil Gowan River, called the Rotoiti by early European settlers, flows quietly out of Lake Rotoroa.

Above:
After leaving Lake Rotoroa, the Gowan gathers speed on its way to join the mighty Buller River.

Above:
The fog clears as the sun brightens Murchison, 131 kilometres south-west of Nelson at the confluence of the Buller and Matakitaki rivers. Named after celebrated Scottish geologist Sir Roderick Impey Murchison, the town faded after its heyday as a gold mining settlement, but has been reborn as a major kayaking centre.

Opposite:
The impressive Maruia Falls on the Maruia River are a result of the major earthquake that struck the Murchison area about 10.20 a.m. on Monday 17 June 1929 and killed 17 people. Originally the water poured over a 1-metre drop but erosion since then has eroded the riverbed further and the torrent has grown.

Above:
Winter snow still covers the shady ground alongside the Buller River, which rises in Lake Rotoiti and flows west for almost 170 kilometres to enter the Tasman Sea at Westport. The river takes it name from British parliamentarian Charles Buller, who was a director of the New Zealand Company.

Letter boxes do not have to be boring.

Above:
Inquisitive Jersey calves at Waimea West.

Opposite:
Designed by the explorer Thomas Brunner, in memory of Francis Horniblow Blundell, St Michael's Anglican Church at Waimea West was built in 1866. In its churchyard are the graves of Nelson's third bishop, the man who reputedly first ploughed South Island soil, and other well-known pioneers.

Above:
Children feeding tame eels at the Jester House Café in the Tasman district.
The eels live in the stream below the bridge to the café, waiting to be fed.

The clay found in the Nelson area is especially good for pottery and the region is rich in potters.
Top left, Charles Shaw 'throws' a pot at his Manuka Pottery in Nelson.
Top right, exotic pieces by Paul Laird of Tahunanui's Waimea Pottery, with the blue of Tasman Bay in the background.
Bottom right, the soft, almost translucent colours of Stephen Robertson's work, displayed at his Mapua pottery.

Above:
The town of Motueka – the name means clump of trees with weka – lies 54 kilometres north-west of Nelson, in an area important for hops, pip fruit, grapes, crafts and market gardens. Motueka is within a short drive of Kaiteriteri Beach, Marahau and the Abel Tasman and Kahurangi National Parks. Some 12,000 people live in Motueka, Moutere and the surrounding townships.

Above:
Parents and children gather for Saturday morning rugby at Riwaka, 5 kilometres from Motueka. Riwaka is a corruption of Riuwaka, meaning the interior of a canoe.

Above:
The salt air has not been kind to this old tractor, parked at Port Motueka.

Above:
Travelling economy class – dogs lined up on the back of a truck at Motueka.

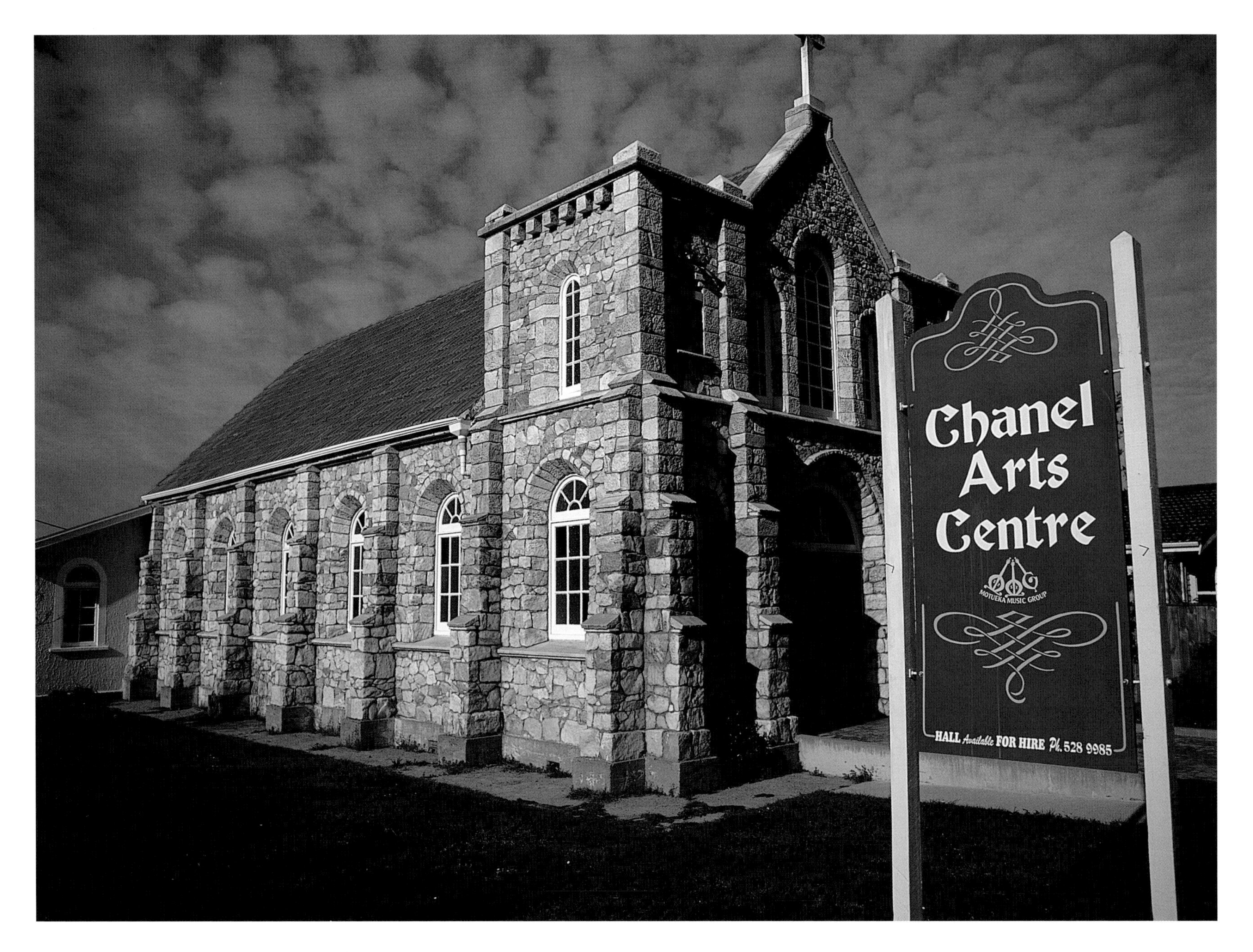

Above:
The Chanel Arts Centre in Motueka, headquarters of the local music group, has made use of a handsome old church.

Above:
Luscious fruit is a trademark of the Motueka area. Visitors enjoy the opportunity to pick their own sun-warmed strawberries.

Fertile soils and a kind climate make Riwaka idea fruit-growing country. Orchards abound and the produce is on sale.

Opposite:
The clear jewel-like greens of the Riwaka Resurgence, where the Riwaka Stream emerges from beneath the Takaka Hill, after flowing underground for 4 kilometres. The cave is popular with divers.

Opposite:
The golden sands and blue waters of Kaiteriteri Beach, 12 kilometres north of Motueka, are a magnet for summer holidaymakers from all over the South Island, and across Cook Strait. The name is a misspelling of Kaiteretere, meaning to eat hurriedly, on the run. A group of Maori having a meal on one of the beach's islands were disturbed and ran to their canoes, taking their food with them and later eating it on their way back to their pa. Kaka Point, at the northern end of the beach, was once a fortified Maori lookout.

Above:
Making sandcastles on Kaiteriteri Beach. Permanent real estate in this area is rather more expensive.

Above:
A myriad of blues and greens in the limpid sea at Kaiteriteri. As the tide flows out of the estuary, it provides more water to frolic in.

Above:
Carrying their shoes, visitors land at Kaiteriteri Beach after a day's walk in Abel Tasman National Park. The smallest of New Zealand's national parks, at 22,139 hectares, it is also the sunniest and warmest – and one of the most beautiful and popular.

Opposite:
Split Apple Rock in Abel Tasman National Park in late afternoon light, with Tasman Bay beyond.

Right:
Rocks like giant fruit inside a cave near Split Apple Rock.

Above:
This Marahau signpost makes a handy lookout for a pair of seagulls. On the estuary of the Marahau River, at the southern end of Abel Tasman National Park, Marahau is 19 kilometres north of Motueka. The name means garden of wind.

Above:
At Marahau's Arts Unique Gallery, Chris (left) and Paul (right) create distinctive carvings from tree stumps and trunks.

Above:
Tractors used for launching kayaks and tourist boats wait at Marahau for their clients to return from a day on the water.

Opposite:
The long summer days bring hordes of tourists from all over the world to paddle kayaks across the still and lovely waters of Abel Tasman National Park. Here several kayakers set off from Marahau for expeditions that may last a day or several days. Kayaking is one of the most popular pastimes in the park.

Above:
At Marahau horse trekkers make their way through an incoming tide.

Above:
This bridge at Marahau marks the start of the 51-kilometre Abel Tasman Coastal Track, which ends at Totaranui. It usually takes 3 to 4 days to walk the full length of the track.

Above:
Idyllic Te Pukatea Bay is one of the drop-off beaches for those doing a day walk on part of the Abel Tasman Coastal Track.

Opposite:
At Torrent Bay, where some lucky bach owners can holiday whenever the mood takes them, the Abel Tasman Coastal Track goes along the beach.

Above:
At full tide kayakers can paddle up the slow-moving Falls River beneath a swingbridge on the Abel Tasman track.

Above:
The Tonga Arches are white against the darkness of the bush. At certain tides it is possible to paddle a kayak between these rocks.

Opposite:
Seals, part of a colony on Tonga Island, rest on rocks in the early morning light.

Above:
Red sky at morning, shepherd's warning – a fiery sunrise over the Tonga Roadstead is a sign of rain to come.

Above:
Golden Onetahuti Beach is another dropping off place for day trampers covering just a section of the Abel Tasman track.

Opposite:
A kayaker celebrating a special occasion enjoys the sunshine and peaceful waters near Tonga Island.

Above:
South Island pied oystercatchers (*Haematopus finschi*) or torea take to the air in Abel Tasman National Park. These birds form large flocks at river estuaries and on tidal flats.

Above:
Shags are black dots on the pale mass of Cottage Loaf Rock. Only a skilled and intrepid climber could have placed the cairn of rocks on top of this distinctive coastal formation.

Above:
Only at low tide can walkers cross Awaroa Inlet. As well as stunning sandy beaches, Awaroa boasts a luxury lodge, a small group of tiny baches, a Department of Conservation (DOC) hut and an airstrip.

Above:
Boats drawn up on the beach at Awaroa Inlet provide access for bach owners at high tide.

Opposite:
Golden Totaranui Beach, 30 kilometres east of Takaka, is the end or beginning point for the Abel Tasman Coastal Track. A large DOC camping ground caters for the many visitors who come here each year. Totaranui means many trees.

Above:
'Me and my shadow' – early morning, Totaranui Beach.

Above:
The long, winding road over Takaka Hill takes drivers through a spectacular and ancient granite and marble landscape, and the views from the summit are memorable.

Above:
Beech trees (*Nothofagus* spp.) line the start of the Takaka Hill Walkway, which runs through marble rock formations, native forest and open shrubland. The full walk, which runs through a working farm, takes two and a half to three hours. It is not difficult but requires care in wet, windy and misty weather. The giant carnivorous snail *Powelliphanta* is found here.

Opposite:
The weird shapes of the marble karst landscape on Takaka Hill have been formed by the weathering of New Zealand's oldest rocks, created when layers of shells, laid down under the sea, were compressed, heated and uplifted. The hill contains some of New Zealand's deepest caves.

Above:
Takaka, the main business, service, shopping and tourist accommodation centre for Golden Bay, was founded in 1854. The town's Maori name means bracken (*Pteris esculentum*). High sunshine hours and abundant rainfall make this superb dairying country.

Left:
This Takaka resident calls himself the Wizard of World's End, referring to long Farewell Spit at the top of the South Island.

Above:
In 2000 the talents of almost 50 people went into the painting of this striking mural in Takaka.

Right:
In a half-day trip the Pupu Hydro Walkway offers a mixture of stunning scenery, fascinating history and plant and bird life, and engineering achievement. A 3-kilometre water race built in 1901–02 gave gold sluicers sufficient pressure to do their work, until the area was abandoned in 1910. A small hydro-electric station built in 1929 and closed in 1981 has been preserved and restored by the Pupu Hydro Society. Visitors can enjoy the song of tuis and bellbirds and the heavy whoosh of wood pigeons and admire the beautiful aqueduct that is part of the hydro development.

Opposite:
The almost unbelievably crystalline waters of the Te Waikoropupu (Pupu) Springs are perhaps Golden Bay's most famous tourist attraction. Overlaying the marble of Takaka is a thick layer of sandstone which, in the Waikoropupu Valley, has been eroded to a point where the underground water has burst through to emerge as New Zealand's largest springs system (and among the 100 biggest in the world). The water temperature is always 11.7°C.

Above:
The maze of limestone formations in Labyrinth Rocks Park near Takaka would not be out of place in one of Peter Jackson's *Lord of the Rings* films.

Opposite:
Deep blue water draws the eye through the road tunnel at Tarakohe Harbour near Takaka.

Above:
This suspension footbridge across the Wainui River near Takaka is sturdier than it looks. The water far below must find its way around huge blocks of granite. The bridge leads to the Wainui Falls, a few minutes' walk away.

Above:
An especially hard granite obstacle has caused the Wainui River to plunge as the Wainui Falls, which are particularly impressive after heavy rain. The surrounding vegetation is marvellously lush, with nikau palms, tree ferns and rata.

Above:
At sunrise a mountain tarn in Kahurangi National Park becomes a sheet of molten red. Opened in May 1996, Kahurangi is one of New Zealand's newest national parks and, at 452,002 hectares, its second largest after Fiordland. The name has a number of meanings, including the apt 'treasured possession', which perfectly describes its mixture of wild rivers, high plateaux and alpine herbfields, and coastal forests. Kahurangi stretches from the base of Farewell Spit in the north to Murchison in the south, the Heaphy River in the west and Tapawera in the east. Motueka, Takaka, Karamea, Tapawera and Murchison are the park's gateway towns.

Above:
Rich early morning light strikes bare slopes high in Kahurangi National Park.

Above:
Mountain tussock aglow at sunrise.

Above:
Lake Cobb. Carved by glaciers, the Cobb Valley in Kahurangi National Park is reached by the challenging and narrow Cobb Dam Road, which winds through amazing scenery as it follows the Takaka River. The small 32 MW Cobb River Power Station, at the junction of the Takaka and Cobb rivers, was built some 50 years ago. Water for the station is taken from the Cobb River, which starts as the outlet of Lake Cobb, high in the Tasman Mountains and flows for 12 kilometres until eventually draining into the artificial Cobb Reservoir, formed when the river was dammed. The Cobb Valley Track runs up the river valley, which contains 540 million-year-old fossils, the oldest ever found in New Zealand.

Above:
The 1152-metre Twins and other peaks of the Braeburn Range are stunning under the first snows of winter. The Twins are also sometimes known as Novara Peak, after the Austrian warship that brought writer and geologist Ferdinand von Hochstetter (1829–84) to New Zealand.

Opposite:
Snow dusts 1795-metre Mount Arthur, on the eastern boundary of Kahurangi national park, and the Tablelands, a high plateau at the heads of the Leslie and Takaka rivers. Beneath the peak is the 700-metre-deep Nettlebed cave system, said to be the deepest in the Southern Hemisphere. Unusually, cavers enter the system from the bottom and work their way up. Thomas Salisbury was the first European to sight the Tablelands, in 1863. There was a gold rush in the area not long afterwards but no big finds were made.

Left:
A mountain astelia (*Astelia nervosa*) takes centre stage among tussock grass on the Mount Arthur Tablelands. This part of Kahurangi National Park has a good system of tracks and huts.

Above:
The little settlement of Bainham in Kahurangi National Park is home to one of New Zealand's most famous shops. Built by two farmers, at a cost of £47, Langfords Store was opened in 1928 by former dairy farmer Edward Bates Langford and his wife Eleanor. Langford had been the local postmaster, from 1924, and also sold some stationery and ran a printing press before turning to full-time retailing. Present owner Lorna Langford began working in the store in 1947 and took over the business in 1952. Her visitors' book is filled with signatures from all over the world, penned by people en route from Nelson to the Heaphy Track, which starts some 14 kilometres away. Bainham takes its name from a combination of the surnames of the two first settlers, Bain and Graham.

Opposite:
The Brown River at the start of the Heaphy Track. Named after 19th-century artist, explorer and soldier Charles Heaphy (1820–81), who made a number of journeys in the district, the track is one of New Zealand's 'Great Walks'. Following a route first followed by James Mackay in 1860, the Heaphy Track runs for 82 kilometres to the West Coast, where it ends 16 kilometres from Karamea. Thousands of people, insect repellent on hand to combat voracious sandflies, make the walk every year.

Above:
The Perry Saddle Hut at the Collingwood end of the Heaphy Track is dwarfed by the immensity of the landscape. The Gouland Downs lie in the distance.

Opposite:
On the Heaphy Track, looking southwards across the open red tussock country of the Gouland Downs. These are named after Collingwood magistrate Henry Gouland, who intended to establish a sheep run here.

Above:
Collingwood, the closest town to Farewell Spit, and the Heaphy Track, was originally a Maori pa at the mouth of the Aorere River. Europeans were building boats there by 1842 and the Pakeha settlement that grew up was originally known as Gibbstown, but later rechristened Collingwood, in honour of Nelson's second in command at the Battle of Trafalgar. During the gold rushes of the 1860s Collingwood boomed – there was even talk of making it the nation's capital – but when the miners went the town faded away. Despite fires in 1859, 1904 and 1967, old Collingwood buildings have survived and the town is full of historical interest.

Above and opposite:
Contrasting beaches near Collingwood – the precision of wave-made ripples on sand and a variety of warm-coloured boulders.

Above:
The Anaweka River enters the Tasman Sea on Nelson's west coast north of Kahurangi Point.

Above:
Alongside the wide, shallow Paturau River, south of Whanganui (Westhaven) Inlet on the west coast. The drive around the inlet's many indentations is best done at high tide. The rivermouth is excellent for whitebaiting. Whanganui, the second largest estuary in the South Island, is rich in wildlife and important for fishing. Its south-westerly end is a marine reserve; the north-eastern two-thirds is a wildlife management reserve.

Above:
Sand Hill Creek runs into the booming surf of the Tasman Sea on Nelson's remote west coast, south of Whanganui Inlet. Lake Otuhie is a splash of sapphire in the background.

Opposite:
The extensive pewter-coloured mudflats of the Whanganui Inlet are exposed at low tide.

Above:
Golden late afternoon light, Whanganui Inlet.

Above:
Massive sand dunes, to the right, are piled up on the wild seaward side of the Whanganui Inlet.

Opposite:
Set in a forested reserve to the north-west of Whanganui Inlet, the two Kaihoka lakes were created when wind-blown sand dunes advanced inland from the coast and cut off the drainage from several small valleys. Plentiful nikau palms among the surrounding bush add a subtropical favour to the area.

Above:
Archway Island from Wharariki Beach, which abounds in extraordinary formations created by the action of wind and wave.

Opposite:
Stone arch, Wharariki Beach.

Above:
Terns are flashes of white against the dark, forbidding cliffs of Wharariki, a true West Coast beach, wild and windswept.

Above:
Persistent onshore winds have sculpted these trees near Farewell Spit.

Opposite:
The sea cliffs of Cape Farewell, the northernmost point of the South Island. The black dots on the rocks at the bottom left are basking seals.

Above:
The spectacular cliffs of Cape Farewell with, in the background, the long curve of Farewell Spit, which stretches from Fossil Point, near Puponga, across the entrance to Golden Bay. At 35 kilometres, it is New Zealand's longest spit composed entirely of sand, which is formed from eroded West Coast granites, schists and other sands that drift north. About 800 metres wide, the spit is built of shifting sand dunes up to 20 metres high. Low scrub, marram grass, lupins and raupo are the principal vegetation. Farewell Spit, which is a nature reserve administered by DOC, is one of New Zealand's most significant habitats for wading birds, especially knots and godwits which, remarkably, fly annually all the way from Alaska.

Above:
Two companies run excursions to the end of Farewell Spit, where a lighthouse has stood since 1870. Positioned 29.5 metres above sea level, it flashes every 15 seconds, the light visible for 24 kilometres. But the spit has caused several wrecks: the last major one was the *Helena* in 1885.

Following page:
Inter-tidal rushes between Puponga and Pakawau. Puponga was the site of a coal mine, opened in 1899, and by the early 20th century hundreds were living in the settlement. After the first mine was closed by flooding and a strike in 1916, smaller seams were worked and despite a resurgence from the late 1950s all mining ceased in the early 1970s. Today there is little to be seen of Puponga's former life as a thriving coal mining town.

GREYSCALE

BIN TRAVELER FORM

Cut By____IRENC____ Qty__37__ Date________

Scanned By______________ Qty______ Date________

Scanned Batch IDs

Notes / Exception